Trust Loops in Leadership

Trust Loops in Leadership

A Primer on Synergy for the Learning Manager

၄

Paul Ludwick

iUniverse, Inc.
New York   Lincoln   Shanghai

Trust Loops in Leadership
A Primer on Synergy for the Learning Manager

iUniverse books may be ordered through booksellers or by contacting:

iUniverse
2021 Pine Lake Road, Suite 100
Lincoln, NE 68512
www.iuniverse.com
1-800-Authors (1-800-288-4677)

ISBN-13: 978-0-595-35520-4 (pbk)
ISBN-13: 978-0-595-80007-0 (ebk)
ISBN-10: 0-595-35520-X (pbk)
ISBN-10: 0-595-80007-6 (ebk)

Printed in the United States of America

To my daughter, Angela, who understands more about the importance of valuing employees than all but a handful of the professional managers I have known. Imagine my surprise when I found out that she had actually been listening to me ramble for all those years. And to my wife, Brenda, who supported me during the times that I worked for managers who didn't get it.

CONTENTS

Preface ix

Acknowledgments xi

Introduction xiii

Section I: Develop Trust Loops

Chapter 1:   What's Coming? 3

Chapter 2:   Invite and Expect Full Participation 6

Chapter 3:   The Vision No One Will Believe 9

Chapter 4:   The Power of Your Own Performance Plan 11

Chapter 5:   Admit Your Own Fallibility 14

Chapter 6:   Fix the Problem, Not the Blame 18

Chapter 7:   Diversity in the Workplace 21

Chapter 8:   Train Liberally 23

Chapter 9:   Say Thank You a Lot 25

Chapter 10:   Who Sets the Goals? 29

Chapter 11:   Responsibility and Authority 31

Chapter 12:   When to Change the Job Description 33

Section II: The Team

Chapter 13:   The Team Is the Key 37

Chapter 14:   Manage the Relationships 40

Chapter 15:   When the Team Does Well 44

Chapter 16:   Vacancies 47

Section III: Make Your Focus a Conscious Choice

Chapter 17:   A Matter of Focus 55

Chapter 18:   Reinventing Yourself 62

Conclusion: Your Mission, Should You Choose to Accept It 65

Index 67

PREFACE

It is my hope that this book will find its way into the genre of what I think of as "airport newsstand management books." You know the ones I mean: books like Robert Townsend's *Up the Organization*, Patrick Lencioni's *The Four Obsessions of an Extraordinary Executive*, and Spencer Johnson's *Who Moved My Cheese?* These are short books that are picked up in airport bookstores because they are quick reads on business flights. But the insights of these books change the manager who comes back from the trip with a new way of looking at the workplace and the work group. That's want I want *Trust Loops in Leadership* to do for managers and workers. I want every manager in the world to see the people with whom they work as willing collaborators in the success of their organization.

In the early 1990s, I began to change my relationship with the people who reported to me. I had made some very bad hiring decisions in the early part of my supervisory career and decided to involve the work group in the interview process to compensate for some of my blind spots. Over the next few years, I began to realize that my entire approach to the way I worked had changed. I had begun by inviting the work group to participate in the hiring process. The result had been greater success in the performance of the entire group. As the group began to realize that I trusted their participation, they became more confident and more committed to all of their work. As they became more committed and more confident, I trusted and involved them more directly in other challenges, like budget crises, goal setting, and new program development. We were developing "trust loops." Success in the new challenges added to their confidence and competence and, at the same time, increased my trust in them. The trust loops became self-perpetuating.

Involving the group in the hiring process is still the way I prefer to begin establishing trust loops, but there are others. This book will show you the specific opportunities to be the one who trusts first. People will respond. You will be gratified by their responses and will trust them more. You will soon find that you spend less time putting out fires and more time looking for the next opportunity for the success of this increasingly competent group of coworkers.

ACKNOWLEDGMENTS

This book comes first and foremost out of a short assignment I had in 1999 as an interim director for the Municipal Court in Scottsdale, Arizona. The assignment gave me a chance to consider and practice everything that I had learned in twenty years about managing work groups. So I want to begin by acknowledging Neal Shearer for giving me the opportunity and the confidence to try and Judge Joe Olcavage for letting me help him manage the city court through a very traumatic transition. With only one exception, what I have learned about managing groups has come from mentors rather than authors, and I need to say thank you to some folks.

To Gordon Pedrow for empowerment, Gladys Baer for the importance of the team, Gloria Olaya for the *second set of eyes*, Neal Shearer for envisioning, Dick Bowers for values and guiding principles, and to John Maltbie and Sam Kathryn Campana for modeling risk. To the staff members of the Neighborhood Revitalization Department in Glendale, Arizona, and the city court in Scottsdale for letting me practice on them. To the staff of the Community Assistance Office in Scottsdale for sharing with me the most exciting five years of my working career. To Rick Canas for helping me explore the reasons why managers who focus on the people who work for them are not typically successful in their rise in an organization.

Now, I need to acknowledge one author. In her book, *Leadership and the New Science,* Margaret Wheatly provided a whole new set of metaphors for effective relationships in the workplace. I hope she was complimented when I asked for her autograph and the book that I handed her had highlights and margin notes on almost every page.

Finally, I need to acknowledge the people who read the drafts, listened to my constant updates, and gave me the feedback I needed to bring this book to publication: Mark Bethel, Decima Sever, Dan Schmidt, Diane Kallal, and Mary Ann Sola.

If this book is helpful to you, I want you to know that these are the people from whom I have learned. Please share my gratitude to them.

INTRODUCTION

In August of 1999, I had come to a breathing space in my job as the community assistance manager for Scottsdale, Arizona. I was not thinking of looking for another job. I was having more fun at work than I had had in a number of years, and the city council had just adopted its first affordable housing strategy, so I had plenty of work out in front of me. The staff of the Community Assistance Office was the strongest group of professionals I had yet to work with, and we were getting ready to take on the management of two additional funding sources that promised to add challenges to the coming year. A major milestone had been crossed, and the new responsibilities would not hit until November.

On that particular day I needed a new challenge to get me moving for a couple of months. And on that day Neal Shearer, the human resources administrator, called and asked if I would consider taking an assignment with the Scottsdale city court. They had lost their presiding judge, the court director, and a key supervisor within the space of a couple of weeks. The acting presiding judge was in need of assistance until key vacancies could be filled. The loss of most of the top management had created serious trauma within the fifty plus employees, and morale was very low. The employees were acting like they had been attacked and were exhibiting a high degree of vulnerability. I had had some prior experience with work groups that had been traumatized by the departure of a manager. And my current work group had a good reputation for knowledge and performance, hence the reason for my being asked to consider a temporary assignment as the acting court director.

Other people who I liked and respected were being asked to consider the assignment as well. But everyone knew it was going to be a tough experience, and no one would feel bad if they didn't get invited to this party.

I had two reasons for wanting to accept the position and work in the court for a few months:

- I didn't know a thing about the operations of a court. In fact, what I did know was that the operations of a court were much more complex than the operations of other city departments.

- I wanted a chance to see if the work group that I was working with at the time was actually as good as I thought they were.

Throughout my adult career, I have been a student of the art of managing work groups for synergistic results. Managing the motivation and relationships of people working together in a group is the most important responsibility of any person in a supervisory role. Approximately half of my education in managing work groups has been the result of learning from my mistakes. I am comfortable with my own mistakes as long as I don't repeat them too often. Since the results of management mistakes are usually painful and long-term, a person who pays attention can learn something over the years.

The outline for this book is almost the exact outline I used for my interview with Judge Olcavage. At the end of that interview, we agreed to work with each other for four months until a new court director could be hired. In my four months of work with Judge Olcavage and the staff of the Scottsdale city court, I had the opportunity to test everything I had come to believe about leading work groups. Everything worked. I thoroughly enjoyed myself, and the staff worked its way through a serious crisis and grew professionally in the process.

This book is intended to serve as a handbook for the young manager who is just beginning his or her first job as a supervisor or for an experienced manager who has again been placed in a learning mode. It is my hope that success in the development of trust loops among the leader and their coworkers will result in a lifelong commitment to the value of the members of the work group in the success of their leader. Both will be happier and more successful.

After I had finished the first draft of this book, I started going through some of the current management literature and found that the style described by the exercises in the book is a mix of transactional and transformational styles. This book has a strong basis in the relationship between the leader and the work group, but it focuses on the way management can change the vision of the group and collaborate with the coworkers to achieve that change.

The style of the book is preachy. I spent five years in a Jesuit seminary. As a result, I am preachy most of the time. The lessons of this book were hard-won—sometimes quite painfully won. At this point in my life and career, I know the value of people in a work group to the success of that group. I do not require you to agree with me, but I will clearly communicate the lessons of my career, and perhaps you'll change your mind. So listen.

Section I

Develop Trust Loops

Any time you want to begin to develop trust loops, there are specific actions you should take that will communicate to the people in your work group that you trust them.

Their response will encourage you to trust them more.

In response, you will involve them even further in the critical tasks of your organization.

Their response will convince you to trust them more. You will become confident that together you can achieve great things.

Together you will achieve great things.

What's Coming?

It is a truism among managers and supervisors that employees are the most important resource. In too many cases, the functional definition of *resource* seems more related to time, muscle, and energy than to partnership in the mission of the organization. Managers who function under the terms of the first definition spend their time herding their employees to accomplish prescribed tasks and complaining about the amount of effort and lack of commitment. Managers who believe in partnership spend their time managing the relationships among themselves and the people in the work group. The work group gets the work done because they can *and* because they want to.

In the next few years, awesome and wonderful change will be coming to the workplace in America. For managers who are not ready for the change, *awesome and wonderful* will have the older connotations of *those terrible calamities before which we stand in shock and despair because we had no idea they could be this bad.* But the manager who is prepared is going to have a good time.

Two events are coming together that will result in drastic change in the workplace. First, the economy is improving. New indicators appear every day. Second, the baby boomers are retiring. In many organizations, retirement parties for boomers are being celebrated on a monthly basis. There will be tremendous numbers of new managers and new supervisors in every office, factory, and government building. These new managers will begin supervising employees at precisely the time when an improving economy gives line employees greater opportunities for movement than they have had for some time. These new job opportunities will come at a time when workers have the added motivation that comes from having spent years in organizations where employees have been treated like they should be thankful to have any job at all. The combined effect of all this movement in the job market may actually be visible in productivity drops in national economic indicators in the coming years.

If you are currently managing a group of people and treating them like they should be happy to have any job at all, this might be a good time to rethink that strategy. It won't be working for you much longer. If you are a first-time manager or a manager who has been more concerned about the work than about the staff and are not having as much success as you would like, some changes in your approach to your work group may help you and your team become more effective and more successful.

For the rest of this book, I am going to refer to the managers, bosses, supervisors, and directors as the *leaders* and the employees, subordinates, and workers as the *coworkers*. Hopefully this will simplify the text and support the message that engaging your coworkers in achieving the vision is essential for your organization and beneficial to everyone involved.

At the most basic level, the employment contract between the leader and the coworkers is simple. The leader agrees to provide opportunities and boundaries, and the coworkers agree to contribute attitude and capacity to accomplish a common goal. That's it. That's the contract.

As the leader, you establish the boundaries and you create the opportunities. Opportunities are financial reward, security, career growth, training, experience, and recognition. Boundaries are mission, vision, performance expectations, performance reviews, audits, job coaching, disciplinary action, and termination.

The coworkers bring capacity and attitude to the job. Capacity includes knowledge, experience, skill, education, temperament, and the physical and mental abilities necessary to accomplish the tasks required. Attitude is the willingness to commit to the needs of the team, the organization, and the customer/client. The common goal is the work. In the workplace, nothing else matters. To the extent that you as the leader manage these things, you will be successful because your work group will be successful.

Start with this functional premise:

> The people who know the customers, the services, the resources, and the problems of the client community and who have the most to gain by providing the best goods and services to those clients are the coworkers in the work group.

Once you accept this premise, the value of the coworkers and your own job responsibilities become clearer. You are responsible for the opportunities and the boundaries. They are responsible for service to the client and to each other. It may require an act of faith in the beginning, but be assured that if you meet your responsibilities, they will meet theirs.

Begin by inviting and expecting full participation of coworkers in meeting goals and solving problems. Create a vision for the future of the organization that no one else believes is attainable. Write your performance plan and hang it on the wall. Admit to your own fallibility. Institutionalize checks and balances in every significant organizational responsibility. Don't tolerate diversity in the workplace—demand it. Train liberally, if for no other reason than it is cheaper than dealing with the cost of ignorance. Say thank you. Say it sincerely, and say it a lot. Manage the relationships, and let the people manage the work. If you are already doing all of these things well, you don't need to finish reading this book. Give it to someone who needs it. You already know people who need it. But if these things sound new and intriguing to you, I invite you to read on. You will enjoy exploring the possibilities.

> **Develop Trust Loops**
>
> *The leader gives clear opportunities and ethical boundaries, and the leader gets improved capacity and growing commitment.*
>
> *The leader gains trust in the coworkers. The coworkers develop trust in the leader.*

Invite and Expect Full Participation

If you want your coworkers to help you make the work group successful, you'd better ask them.

Since it is the responsibility of the leader to provide boundaries and opportunities, it is the obligation of the leader to issue the invitation to the coworkers to be co-owners of the success of the organization. Don't assume that people know they are full participants. They have worked for years in organizations where they have been ordered not to think and not to contribute until told to do so. But as the leader, you can be assured that you have the right to issue the invitation. Once you issue the invitation, there are things you must do to develop the group, but you have to start with the invitation. The invitation takes only one staff meeting. Make it clear that you understand that you may be making a fundamental change in the ground rules and in the way that you and the work group will relate to each other in the future. Begin with something like this:

> "I am not sure how well I have communicated this in the past, but I need for you to know that from this date forward I am admitting that I have no possible way of insuring our success without you. Today I am inviting you to take responsibility, along with me, for the following things:
>
> - Clarifying our mission for each other
> - Regularly identifying dangers and opportunities
> - Working together to constantly improve our potential for success

This may be scary. It may change our relationship a bit or a lot. It may come as a surprise to you that I am aware that I do not have all the answers. It may also surprise you to hear me say that I expect to be getting the answers to critical questions from you and that I expect that you will also begin raising those critical questions and getting those answers from each other.

The reason for this invitation today is that I have come to realize that, while I have some ability to influence the success of our work group, we can improve the group's effectiveness if we work at it together. That is my intention. What do you think?"

8

Just do it.

In the fall of 1998, the Phoenix HUD office called the city of Scottsdale housing agency and told us, "A company has bought a 132-unit senior housing complex in your community and is paying off their assisted mortgage. We want to give you the 132 housing vouchers that will allow the people to stay in their rental units there." This wasn't a complete surprise to us, since we had been working with the purchaser on a plan to finance the renovation of the property, but it was going to increase the workload on one of our work groups by about 25 percent. That was going to be significant. I told the HUD staff person that my staff was really good but that I would get back to her. I assembled the staff and told them what had been asked of us and asked for a plan. They came back to me a few days later and told me, "These people are elderly, and they are going to be frightened at the possibility of change in their living arrangements. We should meet with them as early as possible. Given that we have about three months' notice, we should move up all of our recertification work a bit to clear that month for bringing on those new people. If you will rent us a copy machine that can be placed on site in that complex and if the management company at the property will give us interview space and schedule the people for us, we can do all of the

> *When others tell you how good your team is, it's time for your team to develop a vision that no one will believe but the team.*

certification and transfer work for the renters in three or four days in the most efficient manner possible with the least trauma to the senior residents." Six years later, the Phoenix HUD staff still uses this project as the example of their smoothest, most professional transfer from project-based rental assistance to tenant-based assistance. One hundred thirty-two senior citizens, all of whom had telephone access to the mayor and the congressional delegation in Washington, went through a very complex change in their housing assistance in a period of one week without any sense of disruption in service or personal insecurity in their living arrangements.

I had a pretty good idea that my coworkers were good enough to accomplish this. That was not the important factor. The key factor was that, when asked, they knew they were good enough to make the transition work; and they knew I would be there to support them.

> If you want people to come to a party, you have to send them an invitation.

The Vision No One Will Believe

Organizations need a vision. If people have no idea what their work group is supposed to look like in three, five, or ten years, there is not much they can do to help it get there. Great leaders create visions of great accomplishments for the people with whom they work. In May of 1961, when President John Kennedy appeared before Congress and delivered the speech that directed the United States to put a man on the moon by the end of the decade, he was asking for the impossible. The technology to put a man on the moon simply did not exist. Yet by the end of the decade, an American had walked on the moon and safely returned.

> *The leader needs the group to have a vision for itself.*
> *The leader creates the vision. The work group achieves the vision.*
> *The leader asks the coworkers to create the new vision.*

∞

In 1996, I took a position with an organization that had a reputation for having its leaders leave as a result of audits. The coworkers were extremely insecure and believed that they had no credibility within the larger organization.

On my first day, the person who hired me said, "Sometime soon, tell me what your vision is for this group."

At the end of the week, I called him and said, "Here is my vision for us. It will take us a year to get legal, two to get good, and three to get excellent."

He asked, "How will you know when they are excellent?"

I answered, "When our peers in other communities call us to ask how to get something done."

When I shared that comment with the work group at the next staff meeting, there was uniform disbelief that they would ever be considered "the experts" by people in other communities. Within thirty months, these people were getting their "How do you do this?" calls from other agencies.

> A common vision gives a group something to accomplish together. It's the beginning.

The Power of Your Own
Performance Plan

In thirty years as a municipal employee and middle manager, I don't believe I ever saw the performance plan of the person to whom I reported. Wouldn't it make it a lot easier for everyone in the whole organization if we all clearly understood the performance expectations our leader was trying to meet? Is there any reason why this can't start with you?

Whether you have been in your job for years or for just a few weeks, you know what you need to do during the next year. You work for someone. That person needs to know what your plan for performance is going to be. The common tradition is that the person in the higher position prepares the performance plan, and the person in the subordinate position signs it. As a middle manager, you can change all sorts of dynamics in the work environment

> *As the leader, you need goal-oriented performance.*
> *The leader writes his or her performance plan and shares it.*
> *The coworkers write their own performance plans and help the leader accomplish his goals.*
> *The leader values the support.*

by writing your own performance plan. It only takes a couple of weeks in any position to figure out the general performance expectations. If the organization has a standard format for performance plans, use that for a starting point. Draft your own plan and give it to your leader in the organization. Ask for feedback so you are addressing his or her needs as well as yours. Sure, it will save your leader some work. Your leader won't mind, and it will help clarify both of your expectations about what you need to accomplish in the next year.

Tell your leader that after he or she is comfortable with your proposed plan, you intend to run copies and circulate it to your staff or hang it on the bulletin board or over the water cooler. Sharing your performance plan with the people who report to you is the first step to opening up a trust relationship with your work group. It will:

- Communicate your expectations about your own performance
- Communicate that you hold yourself accountable for your own performance
- Provide a model for individual performance planning

When you share your goals with your coworkers, you help them understand how your goals relate to theirs. More importantly, you communicate that you trust yourself and you trust them. Right or wrong, it is reasonable for people in a work group to believe that the reason that they never see the performance plan for their leader is because if the leader misses one of his or her goals, the coworkers will never hear about it. If you, as the leader, let your people know what your expectations are for your own work, you are giving them power, responsibility, and trust. If you describe the terms of your success, you are also describing the terms of your failure. This is a strong indicator of personal confidence and trust in others.

Sure, you say. But what about the coworker who is just waiting for the chance to figure out what it would take to make you fail? Aren't you just handing them directions on how to make it happen?

Of course you are. But you are also communicating the same information to everyone else in the work group at the same time. And you are communicating to everyone in the whole group that you trust them with this information and that it is important to you that they have it. The vast majority of people in the workplace are eager to repay trust with trust. Your performance plan describes what you are going to do to make your own contribution to the success of the larger organization. You are making the first gesture in the development of shared commitment and responsibility for success by disclosing the terms for your own success for the next year.

Since you are taking the guesswork out of achieving your personal success, an individual can't actively sabotage that venture without the whole group knowing that is what he or she is doing. In many cases, the individual you may be worried about will understand that some self-policing is prudent. In some cases, the pressure of the coworkers to contribute to known objectives will provide positive guidance for the individual. In the worst case, the individual can't claim that since he or she didn't know it was important, there was no obligation to get the work done.

More important, however, is the fact that you have not allowed fear of a potential negative response to keep you from actively enlisting the positive energy of a larger group who want to be part of a successful work venture. In sharing what you expect of yourself, you have given them a template for their own performance plans. They now have opportunities to support your goals and to create some of their own.

> **Take responsibility for your own goals.**

Admit Your Own Fallibility

Everybody makes mistakes. We hear this cliché every day. More often than not, *everybody* means someone other than the boss. Certainly the boss doesn't make mistakes. Or if he does, it is neither polite nor a positive career move to mention it.

But the truth is that everyone really does make mistakes. It is not a question of whether some people make them and some people don't. It is a question of how one handles his mistakes. What are some of the possible ways to deal with an error in judgment?

- Ignore my own mistake or hide it.
- Blame it on someone else.
- Admit it. Own it. Learn from it. Move on.

Examples of the first two methods abound in the workplace. You have seen them all too often. What messages do they send?

If you are in a position of authority and you try to *ignore or hide a mistake,* you may do it because you think you can get away with it or it wasn't that big a mistake anyway. And besides, if you admit to a mistake, the employees will think you don't know what you are doing. This is what you think.

Here is what the people who work for you think:

"That was dumb. I wonder if she knows what a big mess this is going to make."

"Is she unethical or just incompetent?"

"If she or he has to hide mistakes, I guess I can cover up my own so they don't get discovered either. After all, they are just bookkeeping errors."

You are teaching people that a mistake is bad and that it is OK to cover it up if you can. You are teaching people that image is more important than ethics. You just have to read the papers to find the more extreme consequences of this approach to mistakes.

If you are the boss and you *blame other people for your mistakes,* you may do it because it is their responsibility to keep you informed so that you don't make mistakes. That is why you hired them. And besides, if you admit to a mistake, they will think you don't know what you are doing. This is what you think.

Here is what the people who work for you think.

"This guy is an idiot *and* a jerk."

"I need to document every move I make and every move everyone else makes so I don't end up holding the bag."

"If I make a mistake, I have to cover it so deeply that it can never get back to me."

"After all, it's just tax money."

This may be the least productive work environment of all because people are not only afraid of the consequences of a mistake for the organization, they are afraid of the consequences to their own future in the organization. They

---

As the leader, you need to be aware of mistakes in time to correct them.

The leader admits to his or her mistakes. The coworkers admit to theirs.

Mistakes are fixed before they damage the organization. Mutual trust develops.

---

are not just afraid of their own mistakes but those of other people as well. In this type of organization, people keep files on every contact they have with everyone in the organization. These organizations spend more time documenting what they do than they spend actually doing productive work.

People make mistakes every day. The consequences of the mistakes depend to a great extent on the relationships the person has with those around them. The leader establishes the organization's corporate attitude toward mistakes and how they are addressed.

Since mistakes happen with regularity anyway, an entrepreneurial leader doesn't have to wait long to get a chance to model how mistakes are dealt with in the organization.

8

Scottsdale Mayor Sam Campana was not the only entrepreneurial leader in my career, but she was one of the best. She was elected mayor of Scottsdale in the mid-nineties and followed the incredibly charismatic Herb Drinkwater. In the early months of her first term, she had a lot of meetings to attend. When she needed directions to her next event, she would dial 911 and ask. One of the police staff didn't think this was an appropriate use of 911 and filed a complaint that ended up in the media. Within twenty-four hours, Mayor Campana had made the national news.

I had previously worked in communities where the mayor would have tried to have the police chief fired for something this embarrassing. Mayor Campana called a press conference. She told the press that she had made a mistake, had spent an afternoon with the police dispatchers, understood what they were up against every day, and would willingly serve as the national poster child for inappropriate use of 911.

I was new to the organization at that time, and I was completely awestruck by the way she handled herself and by what she had taught the whole organization. The effective lesson was that people make mistakes. When they do, they admit it, learn from it, forgive themselves, and move on. If this is the way the leader handles his or her own mistakes, this is the way everyone else is supposed to handle theirs. The effect of such an action was to release the creativity of a couple of thousand people to attack organizational problems without excessive worry about the consequences of an honest mistake. The next four years were the most exciting and most productive of my career as a public employee. Among other things, we were trying to develop affordable housing in Scottsdale, Arizona. We tried a variety of things. We were lambasted in public meetings. We had many small successes in preservation but none in new development. The important thing for us was that we kept bringing forth ideas. Mayor Campana and the city council never suggested that we stop trying.

You are a human being. You have had some success, or you would not likely be in a position responsible for supervising people. But you are not going to have to manufacture a mistake in order to give your work group an object lesson in the entrepreneurial benefits of risk taking. Your next mistake will come soon enough on its own. All you have to do is be prepared to deal with it. Here are some effective responses to your own failure.

"Yes, I did it."

"It was an honest mistake."

"I really don't want to do that again."

"Here is what I've learned."

"Here is how I would do this in the future."

"Help me fix this, would you?"

"Yes, of course I understand that sometime soon, you will make an honest mistake and we will handle yours the same way. If you keep making the same one over and over again, I may have to talk to you about it. But never worry about the first one."

> Didn't your parents tell you that if you make a mistake, you should own up to it?

Fix the Problem, Not the Blame

On occasion during my formative years as a middle manager, I would respond to a customer complaint or do a spot review on a project and pull the proverbial thread that unraveled the sweater. On two of those occasions, the problem was severe, had involved a cover-up, and had resulted in the dismissal of an employee. Any manager who has been involved in working out one of these cases knows that a great deal of soul searching follows.

The self-talk goes something like this: "I discovered the problem today. Now that I see it, I realize that there have been hints and indicators for some time. If I had caught this problem much earlier, I could have saved myself a lot of work and maybe salvaged a pretty good coworker. How could I have missed the signs when they seem so obvious today?"

> *As the leader, you need predictability.*
> *The leader guides the systems.*
> *The coworkers fix the problems.*
> *The coworkers don't need fixing.*
> *Checks and balances support relationships.*

The fact that there were hints earlier most likely means that the problem had grown to some degree before the person involved started to hide things.

How do you solve problems early enough that they don't reach crisis proportions before you find them? The answer is to institutionalize checks and balances in all of your work systems.

It is time consuming to develop a workplace where problems are dealt with effectively at an early stage. But in the long run, it takes much less time to develop and maintain an open system of checks and balances than it does to staff a criminal investigation or an internal audit.

Problems in the workplace need solutions. As a leader, you can use each problem as an opportunity to institutionalize the checks and balances in work processes. Develop an environment that gets your people involved in bringing the problems forward as soon as someone identifies one. At the beginning stage, you do not have to ask, "Who is responsible?"

You just ask, "How do we fix this one, and what do we need to do to keep it from happening again?"

8

For a few years, Saturn had a commercial in which one of the men on the line described how he or anyone else was empowered to pull the cord that shut down the assembly line if he saw a problem with one of the cars. There wasn't anything in that commercial that hinted that he also had to point to the person he thought had caused the problem and say, "He did it!" He was part of the system that fixed the problem, and he was proud of it.

Institutionalize checks and balances in all of your work systems. Don't just give people permission to stop the production line. Make sure they actually look at the work that has been done by others before the work product moves past them to the next person. Get people comfortable with checks and balances. It takes effort because people have spent more time working in "gotcha" environments than in "helpya" environments. But, as the leader, you have the right to ask the work group to identify the points of harm, and you can help create the points where coworkers systematically look over each other's shoulder. This will work if you model this as a "helpya" step rather than a "gotcha" point.

As you begin to develop checks and balances in your work systems, accept responsibility for asking for and offering help. If you have a field person who is responsible for construction management, make sure that a third party signs off on the final inspection. Make it clear that while you do not need to be that third party for every final inspection, you are volunteering to make yourself available when you are needed. If a payment authorization comes to you without a third party signature, don't authorize the payment. Do volunteer to make the inspection—then have someone else authorize the payment.

Create small do-not-pass points in your systems so that the file/product/process does not move to the third person in line until the second person in line has actually verified the completion of the work of the first person.

The functional reason for checkpoints is that, sooner or later, someone will have a reason to audit your part of the organization. These checks and balances help your organization do well in that audit.

Be willing to modify your systems if something else will work better, but don't eliminate the checks and balances just because they are inconvenient for someone. As an operating premise it is always safe to assume that the person who most needs checks and balances in the system is the person who sees the least need for them.

So what *is* the connection between trust and all these checks and balances? The answer is that systems are not judgmental. If the systems are working, your ability to trust is enhanced, and the coworkers' sense of being trusted is improved because they have a personal role in a predictable system.

> **Fix your systems before you try to fix your people.**

Diversity in the Workplace

While it is critically important in an entrepreneurial organization to be open to mistakes, there is no benefit to having the same mistakes repeated. People who see the world the same way may be able to work cooperatively, but they make the same mistakes over and over—either because they don't catch them or because they don't realize that a particular course of action is offensive or harmful to the mission or the clients. As the leader, you need a healthy diversity of perspective among the members of the work group, and you need for your people to relish that diversity of perspective.

Myers-Briggs work-preference testing is a great way to help coworkers develop a healthy respect for different viewpoints as an important resource in the workplace. As your coworkers begin to understand how different perspectives are actually positive resources for the performance of the group, *different* moves from a perceived weakness, to a tolerated alternate viewpoint, to a celebrated contribution to the successful performance of the group.

∞

You never know where the next good example of a service improvement by a coworker is going to occur. In uptown Phoenix there is a parking garage that serves one of the office buildings. I was leaving the facility one morning a couple of years ago, and I pulled up to the exit booth with my ticket. I was not particularly attentive as I rolled down the window and handed the attendant my validated slip. As he took my ticket with one hand, he stuck a dish full of individually wrapped hard candies in the window and said, "Would you like a piece of candy?"

Slightly surprised, I took a piece of the candy out of the dish and put it in the cup holder and thanked him. We finished the transaction and I left the garage, smiling.

I realized as I drove away that this man had figured out how to be the best parking lot attendant in the world, and it was important to him. I was thrilled to have met him and was a better person for having experienced his kindness.

This man had figured out how to make his job a life-changing experience for people by systematically performing an unexpected act of kindness each time someone drove up to his booth. The people who came to the job after him continue the tradition today. How many office buildings do we leave with a smile in the course of a given workday?

The point here is that, as the manager, you can't know which member of your work group will catch the next big problem in time for a positive solution, identify the next big opportunity, or develop the next great contact. You can, however, influence the environment so that coworkers are aware that differences in viewpoints have beneficial outcomes and that you take delight in the differences.

You will note that none of the discussion, so far in this chapter, has been about racial, ethnic, or gender diversity. Regardless of the racial, ethnic, and gender composition of your work group, manage the group to respect and value diversity of perspective because it improves the odds for success in your mission. If you have demographic diversity already, developing an appreciation for the different perspectives that people bring to the workplace can improve working relationships. If your work group is not demographically diverse and it develops an operating respect for different perspectives, the demography of the group will change naturally over time.

It just will.

> **Delight in diversity of viewpoint among coworkers.**

Train Liberally

For five years, I had a small poster in my office that read, "If you think the cost of training is high, try dealing with the cost of ignorance." Make your coworkers' training plans part of your checks and balances so that when a coworker returns from training, the transfer of knowledge to peers flows naturally from what the person has learned and is now implementing in his or her own work. Training is neither a perk nor a punishment. It is a resource for the people doing the work. Training enhances the capacity and the responsibility of both the person trained and the work group.

> *As the leader, you need competency in coworkers.*
> *The leader provides task-pertinent training.*
> *The coworkers train each other.*
> *Capacity grows.*
> *The leader has competency.*
> *The coworkers gain confidence.*
> *Mutual respect grows.*

Don't send a supervisor to learn the work of a subordinate coworker unless you are sending the subordinate as well. They will learn different things. And don't worry that people are getting too much professional training—at least not in the beginning. Confirming what one knows is nearly as important to professional capacity as learning new things.

One of the benefits of a long career in federal grants administration has been that periodic training has been part of the job. As federal regulations change with changes in administrations, compliance with the changes has made continuing education a minimum requirement for meeting the funding obligations of the grants. In the beginning, everything was new and I absorbed information from the training as a matter of survival. Over time I began to realize that I already knew most of what was being taught, but the value of the training was that I was confirming what I already knew. With that confidence came the beginning of professionalism in my work. Finally, I got to the point where I was doing some of the training. That was when I learned the most because, when you are the trainer, you have to know all the answers. This process of increasing professionalism is what happens with your coworkers as they attend and absorb training and seminars.

Say Thank You a Lot

In the book *Service America*, the author provides a great discussion on the damage that a single bad experience causes to the relationship with a customer. The research indicates that if a customer has a single bad experience with your company, it will take twelve good experiences in order to get that person's opinion of you back up to an even zero.

If you are a manager and have people working for you, you already know that you are creating bad experiences for them all the time.

- The budget has been cut.
- The company is going to be reorganized again.
- The salesman just promised an impossible delivery date—again.
- A citizen just called the mayor's office and complained about you.
- You did not include an important consideration in your project design, and a big part of it will need to be redone.

If you are a middle manager in an organization, delivering unwelcome news like this is your duty, and, in most organizations, it is a pretty frequent duty of the job.

What a terrible dilemma. How can you ever hope to have a marginally positive relationship with your coworkers if you have to give them twelve positive experiences for every one of these bad experiences? You can't give that many raises. It is not likely that your company or organization has the capacity to give that many bonuses.

> **As the leader, you need people who are willing to serve.**
> The leader serves the coworkers.
> The coworkers serve the customers.
> The leader is more productive.
> The coworkers are more professional.

What possible resource do you have that can keep you ahead of the good news/bad news barrier to a positive work environment? You have one, and it will work. You can commit yourself to catching people doing something right and telling them thank you. If you do it often, you will have a credible base to work from when you must deliver that inevitable piece of bad news. Rest assured, it will result in important changes in the way your coworkers respond to bad news or a need to correct a performance problem.

If the organization where you work has an employee recognition program, use it. But don't let it limit your personal recognition of positive performance. Many corporate employee recognition programs have rules that limit the rewards to verifiable cost savings or life-saving heroism. Use the corporate program when it is appropriate, but develop your own method of recognizing any example of personal behavior that you would like to see again. The only rule here is that your gratitude has to be genuine.

8

The first formal thank-you project that I developed was really hokey. I knew it was hokey, and I told my work group about it up front. However, I was convinced that I had a responsibility as a leader to add some positive experiences to a fairly negative corporate work environment. To my surprise, the exercise was really successful.

I got a box of thank-you cards and a roll of silver dollars. Silver dollars were legal tender—not terribly valuable but a little out of the ordinary—and required some effort on my part to secure. I went out of my way to notice specific, positive behaviors that I wanted to see again. When I caught someone doing something good, I immediately jotted down a thank-you note that ended with the words, "I appreciate it. Thank you." Then I taped a silver dollar into the card and gave it to the person directly. If other people were there, I did it in front of them. If no one was around, I just handed it to the person. It was important to me to present the card face-to-face. I wanted to be able to tell the person what I had seen that I liked. It didn't matter to me that it might appear that I was being trivial or goofy. It only mattered that I had seen a behavior that I liked and wanted to see again.

I gave my first thank-you card when the avowed office curmudgeon brought in candy for the receptionists at the front desk. When I would overhear particularly courteous treatment of clients in the waiting area or a kind word to a coworker, I handed out cards. I looked for positive signs of personal initiative or occasions when the accountant simplified a task for someone. I handed out more in the beginning because I wanted to be sure that I was being objective and not playing favorites with particular staff people.

About a year later, I was in the office after hours and dropped something on my secretary's desk. I noticed that she had a half dozen of these thank-you cards lined up on a shelf. The next day, I told her I was worried that someone might steal her cards for the silver dollars and that she could feel free to spend the money herself. Her response was that the cards were important to her and that she wanted people to see them. The following Christmas, my staff gave me a small plaque with the initials of everyone on staff. Below a mounted silver dollar, the engraved text read, "Thanks for your support." It is one of my most prized personal possessions.

Over time, I began to realize that the value I was receiving as a return for these thank-you cards was much greater than the cost to me in time and money. I was telling the people with whom I worked that what they did was important to me, and they were responding by giving me more of the behaviors that I needed to see as a manager. As individuals they were also developing higher levels of trust in me and in each other. The synergy in the work group was beginning to grow.

But wait a minute, you may say. There are all kinds of problems with thanking people. Your *problem employees* will use their own thank-you cards against you if you ever begin a formal disciplinary action against them. People will complain that you gave someone more recognition than they got or that you gave someone else a card for the same thing that they had been doing all along.

Well, you do have to be responsible about it. You have to be responsible for everything you do as a supervisor of other people. Just remember, you are looking for positive actions. You can only recognize what you see. You won't see everything, but you will catch good behaviors with some frequency. You will be getting around to thanking everyone pretty often.

What about the problem employee who is saving these things up as a defense against a future disciplinary action? Recognize positive behavior every time you see it. Documenting behavior or performance for a disciplinary action is a completely separate and distinct course of action every time you have to go through it. Don't worry about someone pulling out a pile of thank-you notes as a defense in a disciplinary hearing. The notes are for very specific actions that you have witnessed. Your position will actually be stronger if you can document that you have recognized good behavior. It will add credibility to your documentation of inappropriate behavior. On the other hand, if you have a documented history of recognizing only those people you perceive to be good employees, a person who has been disciplined may be able to make a case that you have certain, favored employees and that your treatment of people is capricious and inconsistent. In fact, she may be able to demonstrate that you are the guilty party in the dispute over behavior.

Say thank you. Say it a lot. Say it with confidence. Be specific. Don't worry, just do it.

I know your parents told you that if someone does something nice, you should say thank you.

Who Sets the Goals?

8

Most of the people I know who are managers or supervisors were promoted to those positions not because of their supervisory skills but because they were good at staff work. That was how I got my first promotion to middle management. Leaders take the promotion with the confidence that someone must have thought they would be good at it, and, after all, how hard can it be? The thought process goes something like this. Someone thought I was good enough as a staff person that they gave me this job as a supervisor. All I need to do is supervise the people who are working for me in the same fashion that I was supervised by the best supervisor for whom I have ever worked. Unfortunately, there are at least a dozen completely different work styles in the working population. So managing people the way we were most effectively managed gives us about an 8 percent success rate as new managers. Even in the most risk-tolerant organizations, a 92 percent failure rate is not acceptable for very long.

This presents the new manager or supervisor with a horrible paradox. How can you avoid being sued for inconsistent treatment of employees if treating employees the same is not an effective way to motivate them? Is it possible to treat each employee fairly and still treat each one differently? It is not only possible; it is absolutely necessary. Your success as a leader will depend on how well you address this paradox.

People are different. We all know that to be true. We have been reminded of this all of our lives. Until we actually begin to supervise other people and do performance appraisals, we think that means we see things differently from other people. We think, since there is an objective reality out there, the problem is that we have not explained our perspectives well enough. We think that if we take enough time, we can explain it so that people understand. Then we do our first written appraisal of another person's work performance, and they respond. In a single instant we realize that we live on completely different planes of reality from other people. We do not see reality differently—we see different realities.

Acknowledging that there are fundamental differences in the way that people perceive reality does not mean that communication is impossible. You will likely be surprised by the willingness of coworkers to help you achieve your goals if you just tell them what you need.

When you are developing a performance plan or a work plan with coworkers, don't tell them what they have to do. They don't have to do it. They can quit. They can tell you they will do it and then forget or not get around to it. They can give you a whole list of things you have to do before they can possibly accomplish these tasks.

Don't tell them what they should do to become more valuable or further their careers. Your coworkers may not care about your opinion, and they may be right. You cannot control the behavior of anyone who does not give you permission, and you have no right to make judgments about another person's self-worth.

However, you do have a right to your own professional needs as the manager of the work group. You have the right to say to any coworker, "I am responsible, along with you, for the success of this organization. I need the help of everyone in this work group. In order for this group to succeed, I need to ask you to take responsibility for…" Then, fill in the blank.

If you are honest and clear about what you need, you will improve the likelihood that each coworker will accept a personal responsibility to help you accomplish what you need for the good of the organization.

> For your group to succeed, be clear about what you need and why you need it.

Responsibility and Authority

Early in 2004, I attended a city council meeting in my hometown of Mesa, Arizona. It was one of those meetings in which a fairly routine matter gets an odd spin from the press, and a hundred angry and frightened citizens show up to protest a year's worth of work by another group of citizens. The mayor opened the meeting by telling the audience that he understood there were a number of people who had come to address a particular issue, and, while he did not want to deprive anyone of the opportunity to express an opinion, he did want to make sure that people had all their questions answered first. He asked the concerned citizens to go downstairs, meet with staff, select some spokespeople, and organize their comments. About half the people in the room got up and went downstairs. Because I did not have particular opposition to the issue, I stayed and watched the meeting for about twenty minutes before I got up and went downstairs. I was surprised when I walked to the door of the workshop and saw a calm and orderly group of people involved in a discussion that was being led by a couple of staff members who were several steps down in the chain of command. The city manager was standing at the back of the room listening, and the staff members were doing a wonderful job answering difficult questions in a completely open, confident, and courteous manner. The group of citizens eventually returned to the council chambers and addressed the council. One or two of the people still felt the need to grandstand, but the majority of the speakers were quite courteous, and the matter was addressed in about a half hour. I did not agree with the outcome, but I had been truly impressed with the way the council and staff had handled their respective duties. At the time of this meeting, Mike Hutchinson was the city manager. Mike is very active in the community. He regularly attends community meetings, council work study sessions, council meetings, and small group meetings. Two things are noteworthy about his presence in these meetings. One is that, unless you know who he is, you would not know he is the city manager of one of the larger cities in the country. The other is that the meetings are usually led by someone other than a department head, and the meetings are led very well. The people in that organization know their jobs and their responsibilities, and they are confident in their roles. Their competency is a validation of Mike's leadership style.

If your style is to assign responsibility to coworkers without giving them the authority they need to meet that responsibility, do everyone a favor and just do the job yourself. You will get it done faster, and you will be happier with the finished product. There are a couple of essential problems with assigning responsibility without granting authority at the same time. The first is that your plate fills up very quickly, and the second is that your coworkers are no closer to competency in that particular responsibility the next time you consider making an assignment. If you want your coworkers to succeed at a task, you need to give them the authority along with the responsibility. However, there is also a second boundary for this discussion. If you assign authority without conferring responsibility, there is a corresponding likelihood that the outcomes will be contrary to both your goals and your values. The result for you will be the same as in the first scenario—more work for you and no increase in competency for your coworkers.

When you negotiate an assignment with your coworkers, clarify what you expect in the way of an outcome and the amount of authority that you are giving them to accomplish the assignment. Be candid about what you will support, when you want to be consulted, and what you expect in the treatment of other stakeholders in the project. This last expectation is frequently forgotten by people-oriented leaders. This can have the unfortunate result that a project manager will assume the power and the confidence but forget about the leader's values and respect for clients and coworkers. Take the time to address all of the mutual expectations, and then be faithful to your own commitment. Accomplishment will develop confidence, and experience will increase capacity.

Give coworkers what they need in order for everyone to succeed.

When to Change the Job Description

One of the fairly common questions in a job interview is "How long does it take you to become fully functional in a new job?" There are a lot of OK answers to this question. Some of them acknowledge the complexity of the job. Some disclose the confidence, lack of confidence, or overconfidence of the candidate. They all describe the candidate's perspective on a new job. The answers may also hint at the length of time a person plans to invest in the position before moving on. For me, the answer to this question is a very important part of the interview. In my experience with prospective hiring opportunities from either side of the desk, the most preferable increment of time is at least three years. In professional positions, it takes about a year to learn the job, the work group, and the organizational culture. During the first year it costs the organization more to train and acclimate the employee than it gains in creativity and productivity. In the second year, the organization breaks even on its investment of time and money. In the third year, a good employee makes a substantial return on the investment in terms of output, outcomes, and the contribution to the "good of the order." This return on investment is essential to the mission of any organization.

In the interview before a job offer, I put the question to the person something like this:

> I am interested in offering you this position. I need to ask you to commit to working for me for three years. You can lie to me, and I will probably believe you. But if you promise to give me three years, I will promise to try to make this job enough fun that you will want to stay around awhile longer than that. Even if you do not decide to stay, after three years I will consider this to have been a well-compensated agreement on my part.

If you are committed to hiring talented, energetic people who fit well with your work group and its mission, you are going to have periodic turnover. That is healthy and certainly to be expected. The issue with turnover among the talented and ambitious is not whether you can keep them indefinitely, but whether you can make your return on your employment investment as high as possible.

It is a common occurrence in the workplace for the supervisor to wait until a person leaves an important position before that position is reevaluated and reclassified. In fact, the position may have already been advertised and the first set of interviews conducted before it dawns on the supervisor that the job description no longer describes the position that is needed.

At whatever point you realize that you could not replace a particular coworker with the job description or the salary they have now, get the job description reclassified. If you are going to have to do it sooner or later anyway, do it while the person who is doing the job is still in it. If it keeps them interested and productive for another year, you are way ahead of the game. And you know you are going to have to reclassify it anyway.

Human resources staff people hate to do reclassification studies on any positions but human resources positions. But at the point where it is a matter of your own professional self-interest to get a position reclassified, do it. It is always worth the trouble. Please remember that it is your professional self-interest for the work group at large that has to drive this decision. It has to be an organizational need—not the perceived need of the individual coworker— that drives this decision.

Don't try to keep valuable coworkers forever. Just try to keep them longer.

Section II

The Team

The synergy of the team is everything. If a team is successful, even the person who contributes the least is a star. If the team consistently loses, the best player in the world is a footnote in sports history.

The Team Is the Key

Most of what I have discussed so far in this book has been about the relationship between management and the individual employee. All of this discussion has been prologue. The true management miracles come from the team.

8

Gladys Baer taught me almost everything I know about teams. It took her about ten years, and it wasn't easy for her—or for me for that matter—but the lessons changed the way I related to the people whose work I managed. I will be forever grateful.

We have all worked with that one person in the group who looks incredibly productive as an individual but who keeps fellow employees stirred up and off balance all the time. The overall productivity of the group at large just never seems to be what it could be. This suspicion gets confirmed when the high performer leaves the group, and the productivity actually increases. I have worked with people like this on a number of occasions. I used to be very good at hiring this type of person, but that is for a later chapter.

In your personal work history, some of the most rewarding times have been the times when you were doing something as part of an empowered group. The recollection of that experience comes easily and is quite vivid. For some period of time or for a particular project, the work group clicked. The work or the project was in excess of the normal expectations, and you were working way above your own capabilities, but so was everyone else in the group. You didn't care because for some reason, you were having the time of your life.

Then the convention came and went, the project was completed, the funding was cut, or one of the people in the group left the organization. You knew immediately that something had changed and the excitement was gone. You came to work the next day to the humdrum that seems to be the more common experience of employment—with the hope that someday you would get that same exhilaration back again. Maybe it has come back. It does, once in a while, in most of our careers. The experience that inspired you to want to go to work each day was synergy in action. You were sharing an effort with a group of people who were committed to the same goal, who were each holding up their share of the load and acting grateful for the other's contributions. Synergy occurs when the whole exceeds the sum of the parts. When you experience synergy in the workplace, you hear yourself saying things like the following:

"I'm doing things I never thought I was capable of doing."

"If I'm working this hard, why am I having so much fun?"

"You know…We really are as good as we think we are."

"I sure am glad that you are a part of this team."

"I think I may be sorry to see this project end."

"We really *can* be the best at what we do."

The real question is probably not whether synergy happens in the workplace. It happens often enough in a career that most of us remember it and can describe what it was like when if happened. The real question is whether synergy can be extended over long periods of time, multiple projects, and changes in composition of the work team. It is possible if the leader is committed to synergy and is willing to keep focused on it.

What factors operate when synergy is functioning in a team? There probably aren't that many. Think about it from your own experience. The main ones you'll remember include the following:

- The expected outcome was clearly defined.
- The terms of success were pretty clear.
- Individual responsibilities were clearly understood.
- Different talents, perspectives, and approaches were needed.
- Different talents, perspectives, and approaches were respected.
- Necessary resources were reasonably available.
- More than likely, there was at least one deadline.

Wait just a minute here. There are only seven component factors here, and, if you think about it, you could probably break the seven down to three or four. We ought to be working at the top of our capacities every day. We ought to be rolling in synergy. Why aren't we? It's because synergy develops out of the relationships among coworkers, and relationships are fragile.

> The whole is greater than the sum of the parts.

Manage the Relationships

When a group of people with very different talents and ways of looking at the world are working together for a common purpose, there is almost nothing they can't accomplish together. Those of us who have been in the workplace for a few years know this to be true. We have seen it happen on more than one occasion. We have experienced what a connected team can do, and we have marveled at the successes. We have watched with deep regret when teams fell apart, grew apart, or disbanded—either because the project was finished or because someone left the organization. Or maybe there was some fallout among members of the team that did not get resolved. For whatever reason, the synergy was gone, and it was not likely to return.

There are only two components of a successful team. They are diversity of talent and a unified commitment to the mission of the group. Look at successful sports teams. The players don't have the same talents. They don't even have the same level of talent. Different people bring different capacities to the game, but each person is willing to do his or her best to make the most effective contribution they can to the team's victory. But there are also the all-too-frequent examples of teams that have individual players with notably high levels of talent and very poor records of team success. In the spring of 2004, Randy Johnson, pitcher for the Arizona Diamondbacks, pitched the eleventh perfect game in the history of the sport during an extended losing streak. The week before, Johnson had told a reporter that fans would get more for their entertainment dollar if they went to the movies. The perfect game did not change their win-loss ratio either. The team continued to lose more than it was winning for some time. So if you know that the two secrets to the success of the work group are diversity of talent and common commitment, why isn't it easy to put the winning team together? The problem arises out of the inherent tension between diversity of viewpoint among individuals and the personal commitment by these diverse individuals to a common goal. As human beings, we don't readily choose to cooperate with people who don't see the world the same way we do. We go to war with them, consign them to hell, or both. We seldom say, "Wow, I sure am glad you don't see the world the same way I do. I would love to work on a project with you." And yet, that is exactly what the leader of a high-performing team has to say to coworkers. More importantly, the leader has to be able to get coworkers to say this to each other.

You might be thinking, "Well, if I am the person making the hiring decisions, why don't I just hire people who agree with me? Then I can eliminate conflict in the pursuit of the common mission." The answer to this one is easy. When the CEO, the director of finance, and the auditor all see things the same way, you reinforce each others' blind spots and shortcomings. Your company rips off billions of dollars and at least some of you go to prison, while the rest of you wonder, "Why didn't somebody tell me I could get in trouble for this?" Or you are an archbishop of a Catholic diocese, and *everybody* in your work group believes in the authority of the Church and the obligation to forgive completely when forgiveness is asked. As a result of this thinking, you are preparing for a grand jury inquiry and asking yourself, "Why didn't somebody tell me that pedophiles don't get cured by confession?"

Successful organizations don't just tolerate differences in point of view; they value them, reward them, and institutionalize them. If you are a big-picture person, it is important to have some detail-oriented people around you. If you derive your sense of professional satisfaction from balancing the numbers, you may well need people-oriented directors and supervisors to keep your work groups productive.

You may wonder, "So if I agree that it may not be a good idea to have a work group filled with people who all see things the same way, how do I get people with diverse points of view to work together?" Actually, once you commit yourself to it, managing the working relationships of the work group becomes the most important and most difficult duty that you have. However, the side benefit of committing yourself to managing the relationships is that the rest of your work will become easier.

There are five steps involved in moving to relationship management:

1) Become the model for valuing the other point of view.

- Analyze your own personal strengths and tell your people how you think these bring value to the group. Acknowledge that you realize that each person's greatest weakness is the reverse side of his greatest strength.

- Let the group know that you depend on the people with whom you work to have strengths that complement yours. Also let them know that having strengths that complement also compensates for corresponding weaknesses among your group members.

2) Identify the work orientations of each coworker.

- Myers-Briggs is a very effective tool for assessing individual work styles and illustrating the benefits of differences.

3) Talk frequently about the organizational value of different points of view.

- If you talk about it often enough, your coworkers will begin to notice that they actually do depend on each other's differences.

- In time, the members of a truly effective group will begin to celebrate their differences.

4) Never discuss a problem without all of the people involved being in the room for the meeting.

- In my entire working career, I only threw coworkers out of my office one time. It was during a crisis management assignment, and I did not have the luxury of time. Two supervisors had told me that they had a serious problem with the way the coworkers at the front windows were processing money. I invited them to call a meeting—for all of the people who had a stake in the problem—in my office as soon as they could, and we would discuss the problem and develop a solution. At 1:00 the next afternoon, two people were in my office waiting to discuss the problem. The first comment uttered was that the supervisor of the people at the windows was not requiring people to count out their drawers before they left at night. I asked where the supervisor was. They did not know. I asked if she had been invited to the meeting. They said, "No. She was part of the problem that we wanted you to solve." I replied, "Then this meeting is over. I told you when you asked for this meeting that I needed to have all the people in the room. When you have all people together who can possibly help solve this problem, we will talk about it." The next day at 1:00 in the afternoon there were three people in my office, and we began to develop a solution to the problem of balancing cash receipts.

- Involving all of the players in developing the solution to an organizational problem may seem time-consuming, but it is actually quite efficient. Here are some of the reasons why:

  o If people discuss a problem when a significant player is not in the room, the language can be harsh and judgmental.

o You only get part of the story, and it is pretty close to almost impossible to predict the unforeseen consequences of a solution developed in the absence of all the people affected.

o As the leader, you then get to engage in some shuttle diplomacy that wastes your time and fosters mistrust among coworkers.

- When all the coworkers are in the same meeting, the results are better.

o The description of the problem is more objective.

o All of the contributing factors are addressed at the same time.

o Each of the stakeholders leaves the meeting with an understanding of what needs to be done and the consequences of the proposed solution.

o They also leave with a sense that together they can solve a problem.

5) Include tolerance of other viewpoints in performance evaluations.

- Evaluating performance contributions and reinforcing positive behavior is a key to getting more positive behavior in the future.

- Spend time in performance review meetings telling the coworker what his or her contribution has been and how it has made the organization more effective.

- Show him or her, at the same time, how the contribution has been supported and enhanced by the contributions of her coworkers.

- Communicate that he or she is valued individually and as a part of the team—with synergistic power to achieve success.

- This exercise is always important, but it is more critical when the person being evaluated is a talented high performer. These people have tendencies to be judgmental about less-talented coworkers and can have an adverse impact on the overall performance of the group. You can help them to see that the work group has many responsibilities and that different contributions are truly critical to organizational success.

The only thing more difficult than managing working relationships is not managing them.

When the Team Does Well

We have already discussed the value of telling people that you appreciate the behaviors that you hope to see repeated. Just saying thank you is the cheapest and most overlooked resource at the leader's disposal; it is possibly even more effective with the team than it is with the individual coworker.

8

Jim Collins's book *Good to Great* may do more to shift the paradigm on leadership than anything that has been written since Robert Townsend's *Up the Organization.* As I neared the end of the study on those few organizations that had been successful over long periods of time, I was struck by the realization that at several points during the book he talked about the important insights that changed the direction of the research and critical observations that differentiated the good organizations. Collins credited his coworkers individually by name and candidly described the discussion and individual contributions that improved the research and developed the models of great organizations. Then I remembered the photo of all of the people who collaborated on the research on the page before the acknowledgments at the beginning of the book. Collins understands the value of synergy in the successful accomplishment of a mission. Much about this book impressed me. His acknowledgment of his coworkers' contributions impressed me most of all.

It is your responsibility as the leader to communicate the initial vision and the key behaviors that you expect from the team, but it is also your responsibility to notice when there are indications that the team is moving in the direction of the vision. Make a point of being the first to notice the small successes of a team's work, and tell them that you noticed and that you appreciate it. Do this in a staff meeting, or better yet pick a day in the following week to notice these people and bring in pizza and salad. Even if it is coming out of your own pocket, this is a pretty inexpensive way to say thank you. Make it clear that attendance is voluntary, and you don't object if someone has another commitment. Be careful about making too many changes in dates because someone has a conflict. There are very legitimate reasons—as well as the occasional passive-aggressive ones—for people not being able to attend something like this. Don't let a positive act on your part become a source of conflict. It won't be if you make attendance voluntary and let people know that you don't expect this to be the last thank-you event and that you hope they will be able to attend one in the future. Take an opportunity during the meal to let the group know just what it was that you noticed and why you think it was special and that you are grateful. Don't force the team's accomplishment on everyone. Maybe only a few of the team members were involved, but, if it was clearly a team effort that was worthy of note, note it and name the people involved. If you miss someone, and one of the team mentions the support of another team member, thank them for catching the oversight and include that person in your comments. The key here is that you are trying to focus on their efforts together.

Don't forget to spread the word about the accomplishments of your team. Talk about it to your coworkers in other departments and your peers in your industry or professional associations. Success breeds success, and word gets around. When word gets back around to your team that you are saying good things about their work, there is an added confirmation that your praise and gratitude are sincere. More importantly, you are adding to their professional reputation and giving them both confidence and additional responsibility for the reputation of the team.

What is the risk of doing this?

If your recognition and your praise are truthful and sincere, there is almost none. In fact, there is less risk in doing this with teams than there is in doing it with individuals. In a likely but hypothetical situation, a peer in the field calls up one of your coworkers and says, "My boss was talking to the guy you work for, and he said you people really know what you are doing. I have been having a problem with a client (or a regulation). How do you handle this?"

Now your coworker could just say, "Hell, I don't know. I wish he would stop telling people that." But, that is pretty unlikely. Instead, the person will either answer the question, or will say, "Let me get back to you," and will go discuss the issue with another coworker and get back with an answer. All kinds of good things happen in this transaction.

- Your coworkers just learned that you are talking up the team to other people.

- If they are able to answer the question satisfactorily, they gain confidence and confirm their experience by sharing it.

- If they do not know the answer, they will go to a coworker and find out and call the other person back. In which case, they learn from a coworker, reinforcing their trust relationship, and then reinforce their own learning by communicating back to the original person.

- You are several steps closer to your vision of a team broadly recognized for their professional competence.

At some point it time, your work group is going to get outside confirmation that they have achieved the vision that you had for them that they did not believe that they could achieve. On this day, you need to schedule the retreat at which they will develop their own vision for the team. Your only input into this process is that the new vision has to be one that no one will believe but them.

You can help success breed success. Point to it and say, "This is a success!"

Vacancies

Does the following scenario sound in any way familiar? A leader has a vacancy in one of her work groups. She advertises the availability of the position. She assembles some colleagues from similar organizations and gathers them together to interview applicants. She prepares questions to help her understand the applicants' knowledge and aptitude. She brings in each of the applicants for a forty-five-minute interview. She ranks the applicants based on responses to the questions. She checks references and offers the job to the person believed to be best qualified. The new person is hired, introduced to the work group, and begins the first workday with zeal and excitement. Six or eight weeks later, however, the leader finds out that the person is not good with clients, promotes unrest in the work group, and is only marginally productive. The productivity of the whole group has fallen off, and the leader knows the group is in for a lengthy process of training and team building to regain the level of output and effectiveness they had before this new person was hired.

This process of hiring, along with the accompanying results, is one that most managers have used for years. Many people who make hiring decisions still use it faithfully whenever they have vacancies to fill, and, although the process is not guaranteed to fail in identifying the best candidate for the job, it is guaranteed to have unpredictable outcomes. Unpredictability in hiring choices is not an asset in any leader.

For a number of years, many organizations used assessment centers as an alternative to job interviews. The popularity of assessment centers dropped quickly, however, when managers discovered that people who did best in assessment centers were those who were best at role-playing. People who are excellent at role-playing are sometimes sociopaths who have horrible impacts on work groups. So, if the outcome of using a professional interview panel is unpredictable and if assessment centers only turn up the best actors, is there a way to hire people who know the work, are good with clients, and can help the group perform at a higher level? As it turns out, the amazingly simple and provable answer is yes, there is a way.

The way to identify and hire the best candidate for any job is to ask the people who know the job best, who know the clients best, and who know the work group the best. Ask the work group. Involving the work group takes more time than other hiring processes, but it is better to spend time up front and hire the best person for the job than to spend time trying to correct problems later.

> *As the leader, you need employees who work well together.*
> *The leader invites the current coworkers to the interview panel.*
> *The new coworker fits better, is better qualified, and improves*
> *the team.*
> *The team image improves.*
> *Better candidates start seeking positions in the group.*
> *The team gets stronger.*

When done correctly, working with the group to fill vacant positions strengthens the team and builds cooperation and shared confidence between the leader and the coworkers that quickly flows into other forms of problem solving in the work group.

Hiring for Synergy

Before the recruitment process begins, sit down with the work group and identify the knowledge, skills, abilities, and characteristics that the team members feel are important or critical to continuing the work of the team successfully. Do not be surprised if the person described by the team could not possibly exist in real life.

After one or two meetings, the members of the team will sort out the critical characteristics and will recognize that Mother Teresa and Gandhi probably are not looking for employment at this time, and the group may have to settle for someone else. This review may identify certain skills that are needed—requiring changes to the job description or to the job announcement before the position is advertised.

The next step is to advertise extensively to get the largest group of applicants possible. In any hiring situation, it is critical to obtain an adequate group of qualified candidates. In this process, the objective is to find a well-qualified person who also is a good organizational fit. It is likely that this task will require a large pool of candidates. In local governments or larger organizations, this recruitment activity is usually handled by the human resources department. This works fine as long as the department can ensure that the manager sees an adequate number of well-qualified candidates. The next step is to screen resumes for related experience and education. When considering resumes, include applicants who appear to be marginally qualified. In many cases, the candidate who turns out to be the best individual for a job is not the one who looks the best on paper. It is not terribly important to the process whether the work team or the hiring authority does the resume screening, as long as the objective is to get the largest number of interviewees rather than the smallest.

At this point in the process, it is time to bring the work group back together. A few ground rules need to be established. The person who is going to be the hiring authority for the new position needs to be identified. That person will be a supervisor, manager, or superintendent. The work group should be made to understand that its input will be vital, that the needs of the group are instrumental in making the decision, but that the hiring authority, after taking the group's comments into consideration, will make the final decision. If a work group consists of less than a dozen people, everyone in the group should be involved in the hiring process, and several interview teams should be assembled. If clerical staff people are part of the group or are charged with supporting that group, these people need to make up an interview team as well.

Several tasks are important in preparing for the interviews. If writing skills are needed for the position, request a writing sample. Relevant tests should be developed to identify the particular technical experience or skills needed. Each of the teams will develop pertinent interview questions. These questions need to be reviewed in advance to ensure that equal employment opportunity requirements are met. If training is required to make certain that the interview process does not violate anyone's civil rights, this training should take place now.

The Interviews

Candidates who are invited to interviews should be asked to reserve two or three hours for the process. (If the hiring team cannot keep an applicant interested in the interview process for three hours, that person probably is not someone the team would want to hire for a forty-hour-a-week job anyway.)

On the day of the interviews, the clerical interview team should ask a few questions, as well as administer the relevant tests. The other two teams should do separate interviews with each applicant. If the position that is being filled is that of a supervisor, one of the teams should include people from the department, as well as from other groups within the larger organization, and the supervisor for that position. The other team should be composed of people who will be working for the new supervisor. What results at the end of this interview process is four different looks at each candidate. The hiring team has the test material, the input of the clerical team, and the outcomes of two different interviews. Each of these pieces of information will be an important contribution in the overall assessment of the candidates. The technical test is an easy way to find out if the person can deal with relevant information and can communicate it to other people.

The value of the input from the clerical review team is less obvious, but it can be more important. It is almost universally true that people who are patronizing to clients or rude to coworkers also are patronizing and rude to clerical people. Clerical staff can provide valuable input toward identifying the "people skills" problems of some applicants. Splitting the peers and supervisor from the employees provides other information. Any candidate who has a real chance at succeeding in an interview knows how to read the interview team, target the perceived heavy hitter on that team, and play to that person. Snowing a prospective boss for a half hour by saying what he or she wants to hear is not a terribly difficult thing to do. Successful interviewees do this well. The peer group and the employee group, however, are going to be looking for different characteristics and different responses. A person whose only skills are reading interviewers and telling them what they want to hear will run into trouble later when the teams compare notes.

The Review Meeting

The most important part of this hiring process occurs after all of the interviews and tests have been completed. If there have been a large number of candidates, this review meeting may take several hours. In this meeting, all of the people who were involved in the interview process convene and review the various candidates for strengths, weaknesses, inconsistencies, talents, and organizational fit. Often, a person who did well with one group will do poorly with another, and, in the course of an extensive review of all candidates, two or three will begin to rise to the top. Particular concerns of each member of the interview team must be addressed head-on. No one should be made to feel that his or her opinion does not count. It is imperative that the hiring authority be honest about his or her observations on first-, second-, and third-choice candidates. Voting periodically during the process is OK, as long as the team understands that the final choice still rests with the hiring authority. By the end of the meeting, the top two or three choices will be clear to everyone. If consensus cannot be reached, disagreement will be apparent. The areas where consensus does not exist are the ones in which the reference checks need to focus. If someone in the work group has a consistently bad feeling about the top candidate, the reference checks can help to identify whether or not that feeling has merit. In many cases, it does. It may be a good idea to take notes regarding organizational fit. Although organizational fit is a critical issue in the hiring decision, it often is a difficult one to quantify if challenged. Notes regarding behaviors and indications of attitude and work ethics may have value later on. At the close of this meeting, the hiring authority needs to thank all of the participants honestly and make a real commitment to consider all of their input, in addition to checking the references, before making a decision.

The Reference Checks

The final step is to check references. This can be difficult because of prior employers' concerns about lawsuits, but managers who have identified specific behaviors they want to discuss may have greater success in getting answers. Frequently, inflection and the things a reference does not say are important indicators of past work behavior. Once the reference checks have been completed, any remaining areas of concern should be discussed with the top candidate before the job offer is made. In my experience, this process has succeeded in almost every case to identify people who were good employees and good contributors to a work team. The process has been as successful in identifying a manager for a group as it has been in the hiring of peers within the group. Interestingly, this process has resulted in more diverse work groups rather than more homogeneous ones. Apparently employees in a work group really do want the best performer for their group. They will select people for nontraditional roles based on their abilities rather than on such arbitrary factors as gender, race, or disability.

There is an additional benefit that, while originally unintended, surpasses all of the others. When a work group assists with the hiring process, its members have more of a vested interest in helping the chosen person to succeed than they do in seeing that person fail. When a manager uses the traditional approach of hiring and brings a new person into the work group, often the new person makes a mistake within the first few months. The work group communicates either directly or indirectly to the manager that "this idiot you forced on us has screwed up and it's your fault, so you fix it." If the group has been involved in the hiring process, then when the new employee makes his or her first mistake, the group is more inclined to take the attitude that "we thought you were a good candidate for this job, and we need to help you succeed so we all look good."

Does It Always Work?

This process can result in new employees becoming contributing members of highly synergistic teams in a short time. If it fails, it fails because a member of a team, usually the manager, decides too early in the process which is the best candidate for the job and fails to let the process run its own course. It is the responsibility of the hiring authority to keep an open mind about final outcomes—from the initial brainstorming session to the references checks.

> Just ask the people who know what is needed and have the most to lose if they don't get it.

Section III

Make Your Focus a Conscious Choice

You can decide whether you will be a leader or a director. It is the choice between focusing your attention on the people to whom you report or the people with whom you work. Alas, there is a conundrum.

If the focus of your attention is your work group, the workers will thrive and the work group will succeed. However, the success of your work group may not be a guarantee of your personal success and advancement in the organization.

If the focus of your attention is the board of directors or your boss, your workers will get by and the work group will muddle through. However, the lack of success of your work group may not prevent you from advancing in the organization.

The choice is yours.

A Matter of Focus

Some managers approach the responsibility of leadership from the premise that a positive, supportive, and challenging work environment under the leadership of an entrepreneurial, people-centered, and values-based manager is functionally possible and more successful than the work environment under the rule of an autocratic director. However, based on what actu-

> *If every person who has ever been asked to describe the best supervisor of his or her career lists the same traits, why are there so many ineffective managers in the workplace?*

ally happens in many workplaces in America, one has to be honest and ask, "Does a positive work environment really matter?"

If you are an employee in the organization, you probably think, "Of course it matters. I do my best work in a positive environment. I am more productive. I serve clients better. I want to be at work. I spend less time complaining."

If you are the customer, you may think, "I don't care whether they are happy or not. I just want them to do what I need for them to do."

And if you are the citizen of a community, you may think, "If the garbage is picked up and the police show up when I need them, I would just as soon the employees weren't too happy. We don't need to be paying so many of them anyway."

Actually, there is documented evidence that it does make a difference if the coworkers are happy in their work. (Ulrich, Halbrook, Meder, and Thorge. "Employee and Customer Attachment Synergies for Competitive Advantage"; Human Resources Planning, 1991.) Positive treatment of the coworkers is reflected in a more positive experience by customers, which translates into higher levels of citizen satisfaction and higher numbers of return customers.

In the development of this book, one question kept coming back to me. It was this:

If the way employees are treated has a positive result in the responses of citizens and customers, why do organizations more or less routinely alternate between visionary entrepreneurial managers who create excitement and challenge in the workplace and autocratic directors who take all the fun out of coming to work?

One possible but completely hypothetical answer is that there may be a critical weakness in the work group–oriented leader. What actually happens in the council chambers and the boardroom when decisions are made about hiring a new manager? There appear to be real cycles in the management styles of people who lead organizations. Why is that? Why does a council with one of the most widely known people-oriented managers in the country replace that manager with a known autocrat? On the other hand, why does the council in an adjacent community decide to hire a highly nurturing manager when a long-tenured manager with a very controlling work style retires?

Is there a needed correction that influences the decision about the style of the manager that the council perceives that it needs? The weakness of a highly autocratic style is pretty easy to identify. Turnover is higher. Reports about work take the place of actual work. Problem solving slows down, and bureaucracy builds. Sooner or later, a new board of directors realizes that rapid change is necessary for organizational survival. The organization needs an entrepreneurial manager that can involve the whole organization in problem solving.

But if the bureaucratic consequences of an autocratic style must be remedied by an entrepreneurial leader, then what bad things happen in the term of an entrepreneurial manager that have to be corrected when that manager leaves? Is there a way to prevent the bad things so that the positive work environment does not have to change?

An answer may lie in the single inherent paradox in the entrepreneurial management style. The invitation to risk assumes an underlying work ethic that may not be present in every manager in an organization. The entrepreneurial leader has an ethical obligation to demand implementation of the organization's vision by all of the managers in the organization. However, the entrepreneurial leader's commitment to empowerment and risk-tolerance mandates a high degree of trust in coworkers. Hence the dilemma, how does a leader empower people and hold them accountable at the same time?

Maintaining the dynamic tension between empowerment and accountability is the central responsibility of the effective leader. On the face of it, this appears to be paradoxical. Underlying this paradox are several others that are equally important. They are:

- Trusting coworkers while maintaining good checks and balances
- Welcoming mistakes but punishing dishonesty
- Leading and serving
- Supporting the needs of the organization and the needs of the coworkers
- Keeping work fun while still keeping it work, and
- Caring for coworkers without becoming physically involved with them

I own an autographed copy of Margaret Wheatley's *Leadership and the New Science.* It is one of my most prized possessions. A few years ago, a coworker and I picked her up at the Phoenix airport when she was in the Valley to do a presentation in Glendale. At dinner, I asked her if she would autograph it, and she was gracious. I am not sure whether she was surprised or honored when I handed her a paperback copy of the book that was nearly completely covered with yellow highlights, underlining, and notes in the margins. I had read the book several times, and it is still my favorite book on management philosophy.

I still reread the book occasionally. I consider the key insight in the book to be in Chapter Two: *Newtonian Organizations in a Quantum Age.* The paragraph reads:

> Those who are open to others and who see others in their fullness create positive energy. Love in organizations, then, is the most potent source of energy we have available. And all because we live in a quantum universe that knows nothing of itself, independent of its relationships.

My margin note reads, "How the hell do I communicate to coworkers that I love them without getting accused of sexual harassment?"

I said that leading work groups in a truly effective manner involves a number of paradoxes. The one where you really do love the people you work with, without ever actually touching them, is the most significant.

Successful leadership may be described best in the following statement to the coworker:

> "We have work to do together that depends on both of us. I pledge to care about you, to value your contribution, to support you, and to give you opportunities for professional growth and reward. What I require from you is work, integrity, and respect for other people."

The crass and functional translation of this statement is:

> "I promise to love you without touching you and to give you a work environment that can be fun for you—as long as you don't cheat the organization, harass any of your coworkers, or disrespect them or anyone else. If you do any of these things, you won't like the consequences."

Might there be another answer to the question of succession?

So, is the question really that there is some weakness in the demand for accountability in the work group-oriented leader that has to be corrected when it is time to replace that leader with a new one? It is possible, but highly doubtful. As I began to test this theory with other work group-oriented leaders, two other answers presented themselves. First, people don't think much about management effectiveness when they are making hiring decisions and, second, people who are effective at managing work groups are not as effective at managing upward.

The first answer is that the reason management style appears to alternate from one manager to another is that people making hiring decisions about managers seldom think about management style during the search for the next manager. And, when they think about it, the candidate's style of management is seldom as important to their decision as are the candidate's experience with other matters that are high on the organizational agenda at that time. Think about the last time you were involved in selecting a candidate for a supervisor's position. Did their management style weigh as heavily as their accounting background or their sales record or their planning experience? Actually, leadership, which is the most important skill for organizational success is probably the one that receives the least consideration in the selection of a manager. Why is that?

I was ending a long interview with a manager who had impressed me greatly, not just because he agreed with me about the importance of valuing the work group but because of his background. He had had a long history of turning around call centers for a telephone company. He had been good at it. His direction in each one of his assignments had been to "fix it or dismantle it." In each case, his work group orientation had been successful in turning both the morale and the effectiveness of the group. This leader understood his responsibilities and obviously had all the necessary skills. He had validated every piece of advice in this book, and I was pleased.

Then he volunteered, "You know, I have to tell you that I have a weakness."

I answered, "Well, you were doing fine, and I hadn't asked, but go ahead and tell me."

He said, "I am just not very good at managing upward. I am better at managing the people who work for me than I am at managing the people I work for."

At the time, I thought to myself, "Wow, that's odd. I am not good at that either." What I said to him was, "Hmm. That's interesting."

However, he had given me the answer to the key question about management. "If every person who has ever been asked in a job interview to describe the best supervisor they ever worked for lists the same set of traits, why are there still so many ineffective managers in the workplace?" The answer is that, as a rule, people who are better at managing upward do more of the things that get them noticed and promoted to increasingly responsible positions in organizations than do the managers who are better at managing the people who work for them.

It is a matter of focus. And people who focus their attention on you are easier for you to like. That may be the most basic response in all human relationships. We are all attracted to people who validate us by the quality of the attention they give us.

And managers in an organization have to focus their attention someplace. There is choice here, and sometimes it becomes a matter personal ethics. The managers who focus their attention on the work group are going to invest in the coworkers' success more than the managers who focus their attention on the people they report to in the organization. Please understand that I'm not intending to indict either choice. Each choice has value, and each choice has consequences. And each choice places an ethical fulcrum in decision points that are critical to the future of the organization. For the purposes of differentiating these two approaches, I am going to continue to refer to the work group-focused manager as *leader,* and the manager who focuses upward in the chain of command as *director.*

To illustrate, let's look at a completely hypothetical example. The city manager calls a pre-budget meeting and says, "This is a really tight year, I don't want to see any requests for budget increases in this budget process."

The *director* calls a staff meeting and says, "The city manager has told us that this next year is going to be really tight, and she does not want to see any requests for budget increases. I know we have been understaffed for awhile now, and we have been getting more and more complaints about response time, but we are just going to have to pull together and tough it through one more year."

The *leader* calls a staff meeting and says, "The city manager has told us that this next year is going to be really tight, and she does not want to see any requests for budget increases. I know we have been understaffed for awhile now, and we have been getting more and more complaints about response time. Justifying another position is going to be difficult for me to do. But it is my responsibility to do what is in my power to make our part of the organization succeed. Our first responsibility is to keep our service level without an increase in funds or staff, and we need to look at how to do that. If that is not possible, you tell me how badly we need the new position and whether you are willing to help me put together the case for it. Or tell me that it is not worth the effort in this environment, and we will just do our best for the next year. I can't guarantee that we'll get the position if we try, but I can guarantee that if we don't try, we will not get it."

The leader may succeed in getting the new position and may improve the response time. He may also be perceived by the city manager or other managers in the organization as not being a team player. This is always the risk to the leader for placing the greater focus on the work group. The director may have increased response times, more complaints, and higher turnover but may be perceived as more of a team player and more responsive to the needs of the larger organization. These consequences are not predictable without knowledge of the particular culture of the organization. If the city manager's philosophy is that

> *The leader makes the work group the focus of attention. The director focuses attention on the people above him or her in the organization.*

the city council leads her and she leads the organization to follow the direction of the council, then she is a *director* and will see people who follow her direction as being valuable to her performance of her duties. If the city manager's philosophy is that the city council and the city employees work together to serve the needs of the city, she is a *leader* who is going to value the people who are most successful at problem solving.

The individual manager works in a continuum between leadership and directorship and moves back and forth along that continuum. But the individual also makes a personal decision about whether he or she will choose to be a leader or a director. This is the choice that governs the manager's supervisory style and how they behave in crisis. Neither style guarantees personal career advancement, because organizational values and culture change over time and different boards of directors and chief executive officers value behaviors differently.

The purpose of this book has been to provide tools and discussion for managers who desire to build a trust-based leadership style that involves the work group in the success of the organization. It is possible to predict the consequences of that style on the performance of the work group and to ensure mid- and long-term success in the endeavors of that work group. It is not possible to predict whether that success will be perceived as valuable by the board of directors or whether it will result in promotions for the person who successfully leads the work group. However, it is a near certainty that the *leader* will be more challenged and will have more fun at work than will the *director.* The choice is yours.

> **Choose to be a *leader.***

Reinventing Yourself

How often have you heard someone—maybe even the person in the mirror—say, "I would leave this place tomorrow if I didn't have six years left until I can retire"?

If you are unhappy at work, six years at forty hours a week is a really, really long time. Six years is long enough to get really bitter. Six years is long enough for a heart attack. Six years in an environment where you do not feel that you are your best self can have an impact on your self-esteem for the rest of your life. What if the next six years could be the most successful six years of your professional career? Think about it. I mean really think about it.

Organizations change, and so do people. It is completely possible that you and the organization for which you have been working have moved in different directions. It happens. This can be especially true for work group-oriented leaders in middle-management positions. When an organization's management style shifts from a leadership model to a director model, a middle manager with a strong orientation toward the work group can experience a real disconnect with a top-down approach to the work. As an entity, the organization goes through the steps of a normal grieving process, and eventually most people accept the new model and life goes on. "I only have a few years left before retirement anyway, and this place is probably no worse than anyplace else."

The choice to stay in a job that is no longer challenging or a good fit to a personal work ethic may be made for a lot of valid reasons. There may be compelling family reasons or reasons related to insurance, pension, or finances, which eliminate any choice but the "retire here" option. If you have seriously considered all of the options and have consciously chosen this one, that's fine. Go for it and begin to focus on retirement planning, next-career planning, weekends, or vacations.

However, if you are not having a good time because there is a serious disconnect with your personal ethics or because you can no longer insulate your work group from organizational dysfunction, consider the following:

- Organizations go through leadership-directorship cycles.

- Every place is not just as bad as everyplace else.

- Organizational culture is one of the things you assess when looking for a new job, just like salary.

- If you have tried to fit yourself into your current organization or have worked to change your current organization and you still don't fit in the present culture, the only choice left is to find an organization where you do fit better.

- If you are beginning to doubt your own effectiveness or competency, it may be the organization you are in. The only way to find out is to change organizations and see if you do better. If you are careful about your choices, the odds are that you will.

- While you have been working in your current organization, you have been gaining experience and accumulating baggage. You are aware of the experience. The organization keeps track of the baggage. Institutional memory concerning the mistakes people make as they grow is very unforgiving.

- When you move to a new organization, you take the experience with you. You leave the baggage.

- A new job, late in your career, can give you the opportunity to validate what you have learned and can allow you to make a mutually gratifying contribution to a new organization.

Don't assume that the only possible option to a bad fit with your current organization is to stick it out to retirement. You might go to work somewhere else and have so much fun that you are no longer interested in retiring.

Your Mission, Should You Choose to Accept It

Leading a work group is never easy, but it can be effective and rewarding. Invite your coworkers to accept responsibility for the group's success. As a group, they will accept the invitation.

Communicate vision and expectations. The work group will rise to them.

Welcome mistakes as learning experiences. People will grow.

Delegate responsibility, authority, and accountability at the same time and in equal amounts. You will achieve more.

Institutionalize checks and balances. You will get trust and predictability.

Train liberally. Your people will get better at their jobs.

Manage relationships so that the people can manage the work. Your work group will be more successful, and people will stay with you until they are sure that a new opportunity is really better and not just something different.

If you concentrate on the trust loops, you will be a more effective leader of people. Your work will become much more interesting. You will have a great time.

Have fun!

8

INDEX

A

accountability and empowering people, 56–57
admitting mistakes, 14–17
asking coworkers to accept responsibility, 30
assessment centers, using, 47
assignments, negotiating, 32
authority and responsibility, assigning, 31–32

B

baby boomers, retirement of, 3
bad experiences and leadership, 25
blame versus correcting problems, 14–15
bosses. *See* leaders

C

career changes, 62–63
changes in workplace, the economy and, 3
checks and balances to control problems, 19–20
clerical staff and hiring new coworkers, 50
commitment to mission, successful teams and, 40–41
coworkers
    asking to accept responsibility, 30
    benefit of participation in hiring, 52
    bringing capacity and attitude, 4
    defined, 4
    and delivery of unwelcome news, 25–26
    developing respect for diversity, 21
    fixing problems, 18
    hiring, 33–34

keeping them longer, 34
mistakes and, 14–15
need for competency in, 23–24
negotiating assignments for, 31–32
performance appraisals, 29–30
problem employees and thank-you cards, 27
professionalism and training, 23–24
service improvements from, 21–22
sharing goals with, 12
solving problems among, 42–43
template for performance, 13
thanking, 25–28
and trust, 12
turnover, 33–34
value of happy, 55–56
willingness to serve, 25–26

D

directors. *See also* leaders
    versus leaders, 59–61
diversity in workplace
    organizational value of, 42
    requirement for, 21
    and successful organizations, 41
    and successful teams, 40–41

E

economy, and changes in workplace, 3–4
employees. *See* coworkers
empowering people and accountability, 56–57

F

focus of attention, 59–61

G

goals, responsibility for, 30
Good to Great (Jim Collins), 44

H

hiring and management styles, 58
hiring new coworkers, 47–52

I

interviews
    clerical staff and, 50
    and hiring for synergy, 49–50
    for new employee, 33–34
    preparing for, 49

J

job description, when to change, 34

L

leaders
    admitting mistakes, 15
    asking coworkers to accept responsibility, 30
    and boundaries, 4
    creating vision, 9–10
    defined, 4
    delivering bad news, 25–26
    versus directors, 59–61
    employment contract with coworkers, 4
    fallibility of, 14–15
    focusing attention, 59–61
    goal sharing with coworkers, 12–13
    inviting participation, 6–7
    versus leaders, 59–61
    leadership style and hiring, 58
    manage relationships, 5
    managers of, 59
    mistakes and, 14–15
    need for predictability, 18–19
    negotiating an assignment, 32
    and opportunities, 4
    performance appraisals of coworkers, 29–30
    performance plans for, 4–5, 11–13
    relationships and synergy, 38–39

return for thank-you projects, 27
rewarding early team success, 44–45
solving problems among coworkers, 42–43
spreading word about team success, 45–46
steps for moving to relationship management, 41–43
teams and, 37–39
thanking coworkers, 25–28
using coworkers to help hire others, 48
using trust groups, 65
turnover, 33–34
when to reclassify coworker positions, 34
Leadership and the New Science (Margaret Wheatley), 57
leadership styles. *See also* management styles
    focus choices, 53–61
    leaders versus directors, 53

M

management styles
    autocratic, 56
    cycles in, 56
    directors versus leaders, 59–61
    empowering people and accountability, 56–57
    entrepreneurial, 56–57
    hiring managers and, 58
managers. *See* leaders
mistakes
    admitting, 14
    correcting, 15
    fear and, 15
    handling, 16–17
Myers-Briggs work-preference testing, 21, 42

N

negotiating assignments for coworkers, 32

O

opportunities, creating, 4

P

paradoxes in leading work groups, 56–58
participation, inviting, 6–7
performance appraisals, 29–30
performance evaluations, including tolerance of other viewpoints, 43
performance plans
    coworkers and, 30
    fear of negative response, 13
    for leaders, 11
    sharing, 11–12
    work environment and, 11
predictability, need for, 18–19
problem employees and thank-you cards, 27–28
problems
    checks and balances and, 19–20
    diversity and solutions for, 22
    early signs of, 18–19
    fixed by coworkers, 18–19

R

reference checks for hiring new coworker, 51
relationship management, steps toward, 41–43
relationships in workplace
    checks and balances support, 18–19
    first steps in managing, 41–43
resources
    employees as, 3
    thank-you projects and, 26–27
responsibility
    asking coworkers to accept, 30
    and assigning authority, 31–32
review meeting for hiring new coworker, 50–51

S

stakeholders, treatment of, 32
supervisors. *See* leaders
synergy
    defined, 38
    extending, 38–39

factors in, 38
hiring for, 48–52
and relationships among coworkers, 39

T

teams. *See* workgroups
thanking coworkers, need for, 25–28
thank-you projects, 26–27
training
    cost, 5
    liberal use of, 5
    need for, 23–24
trust
    building, 5
    and checks and balances in workplace, 20
    using, 5
trust loops
    defined, 5
    developing, 1
    using, 65
turnover, 33–34

V

vacancies
    assessment centers and, 47
    hiring for synergy, 48–52
    and traditional hiring procedures, 47
    using coworkers in hiring process, 48
vision
    evaluating, 9–10
    need for, 9–10
    outside confirmation of achieving, 46
    for workgroups, 7–8

W

work environment
    the thank-you resource, 26
    value of positivity in, 55–56
workgroups
    building successful, 40–41

components of successful, 40
hiring for successful, 41
and hiring new members, 48–49
paradoxes in leading, 56–58
productivity and, 37–38
spreading good news about, 45
thanking, 44–45
vision for, 7–8
work plans and coworkers, 30

Y
yourself, reinventing, 62–63

978-0-595-35520-4
0-595-35520-X

www.ingramcontent.com/pod-product-compliance
Lightning Source LLC
Chambersburg PA
CBHW030915180526
45163CB00004B/1840